EXTINCT!

Becca Heddle

Collins

CONTENTS

CHAPTER 1

Extinction

This book is about extinct creatures. So what does it mean to be extinct?

Only living things can become extinct. So plants, animals, birds, insects, and creatures that live in rivers and seas can all become extinct. This is when they all die out and there are none of them left.

It sounds sad. But extinctions have been happening as long as there's been life on Earth – and that's over 3.7 billion years.

The very first living things were microscopic ones like bacteria – too small to see without a microscope. Over millions of years, these tiny creatures **evolved** to become better at surviving. The older ones became extinct, and gradually, bigger creatures evolved that looked like ones we have today.

These tracks were left by prehistoric worms. They show us that creatures were big enough to leave tracks we recognise, over 500 million years ago.

The success of life on Earth is all about some creatures dying out, and others taking their places. Sometimes this has happened because new creatures were better at getting food, which left old ones with nothing to eat. Sometimes it's happened because of big changes all over the planet.

These changes affected the living conditions for all the plants and animals on Earth. Sometimes, it just became too hot or too cold for some creatures to survive. This is what happened to the dinosaurs.

Most dinosaurs died out in a big 'extinction event', 66 million years ago. An enormous **asteroid** landed in Mexico. It threw up a huge cloud of dust that surrounded the world. This cloud blocked the sun, making the planet cooler.

The dinosaurs were **reptiles** – they needed warmth to live, so most of them became extinct. And that left space for **mammals** like us to evolve.

The cold conditions that killed off most dinosaurs weren't a problem for mammals. They don't need warmth from outside themselves, so they were able to live where the dinosaurs had lived before. Some flying dinosaurs survived and evolved into various birds.

Closest living relative

T-rex

chicken

There have been five massive extinction events in the history of the world. Each time, more than three-quarters of the plants and animals were wiped out.

Some extinction events made the whole world much warmer or much colder.

At least one event made the water in the seas acidic, like lemon juice – that didn't suit many creatures.

Some of the events were caused by volcanoes, on land or under the sea.

More kinds of creatures died out in these extinction events than are living on Earth today!

These creatures mostly died out before humans even existed – so how do we know about them?

We can find traces of extinct creatures in ancient rocks – like the worm tracks on page 3. And when creatures died in the right places, parts of them became **fossils**, or left fossil prints.

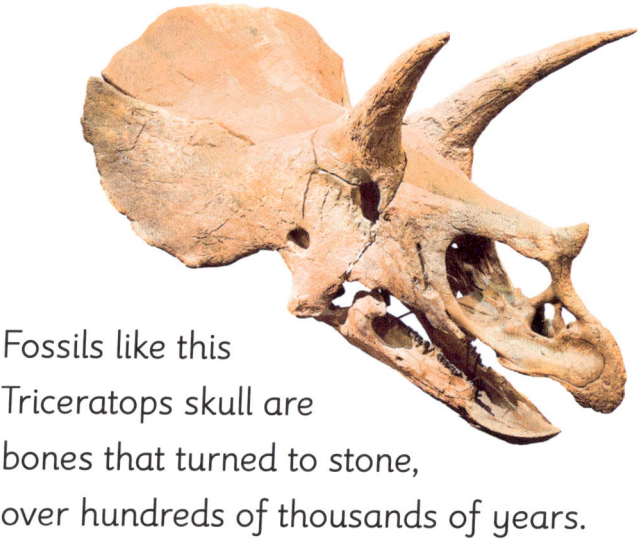

Fossils like this Triceratops skull are bones that turned to stone, over hundreds of thousands of years.

Once humans existed, they left behind information too.

Stone-Age humans made pictures of the creatures in their world. About 2,500 years ago, a Greek **philosopher** wrote about fossils, realising they were the remains of prehistoric creatures. We also know about creatures that became extinct more recently. Explorers have drawn pictures, taken photographs, and collected skins and bones.

All this information helps us discover intriguing life forms from the past.

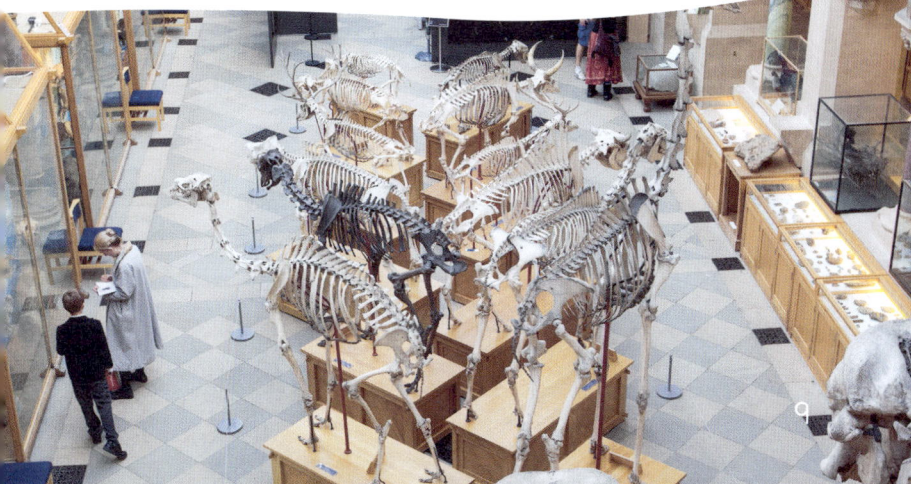

Extinction events timeline

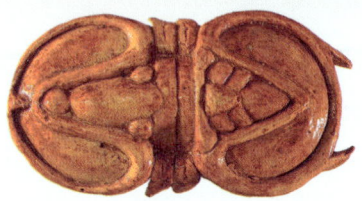

447 million years ago:
Earth cooling, lower seas

252 million years ago:
Earth warming, volcanoes

450   400   350   300

Millions of years ago

378 million years ago:
Earth cooling, new plants

66 million years ago:
Earth cooling, asteroid

200 **150** **100** **50**

199 million years ago:
Earth warming, undersea
volcanoes and acidic seas

CHAPTER 2

Before the dinosaurs

Even before the dinosaurs, the world was full of interesting creatures, which are now extinct.

Anomalocaris were extra-large, prehistoric shrimps from about 500 million years ago. At that time, everything lived in the seas.

Today's shrimps measure 4–20 centimetres, but Anomalocaris were about 50–60 centimetres long.

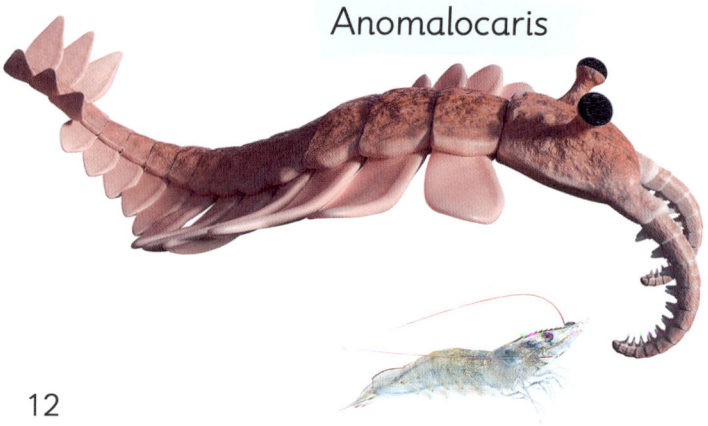

Anomalocaris

Trilobites were very successful **marine** creatures. They lived in the seas for over 250 million years, and there were over 20,000 different kinds.

Some trilobites swam around, some burrowed down, and others walked on the **seabed**.

trilobites

There were so many trilobites, they left lots of fossils over millions of years. So we can see how they developed and changed. Some of them had spikes to guard themselves from predators. Some were as small as the tiniest flies, and some were as big as today's cats.

They all became extinct around 252 million years ago.

spikes ⟶

All of this is the trilobite's eye.

More about ... eyes

Trilobite fossils are the earliest fossils we've found that have eyes.

The first trilobite eyes were crescent-shaped (like a new moon), so the creatures could see all around themselves.

50 million years later, there were many different trilobite eyes. Some trilobites had eyes on stalks, and others had wraparound eyes with more than a thousand lenses. Insects today still have 'compound eyes' with lots of lenses.

300 million years ago, creatures were living on land, including some enormous insects.

Griffinflies were probably the biggest. They looked like dragonflies today, but their wings measured up to 71 centimetres across. The biggest dragonfly today has a wingspan of 19 centimetres.

Put two rulers end to end – that's almost as long as a griffinfly's wingspan.

Griffinflies were predators that hunted smaller insects. They had spikes on their front legs to help catch their prey. We know their prey could be large, because griffinflies had powerful mouthparts to break things into smaller pieces to eat.

They probably lived in **wetlands** and marshes – it would have been hard to fly between trees with those huge wings.

Scutosaurus lived about 260 million years ago. Scientists named them after the bony plates that covered their body – the name means "shield lizard". They weighed about 1,100 kilograms – more than twice as much as a grizzly bear.

Scutosaurus needed their shield plates to protect them from their main predator, Inostrancevia, which had really long, sharp teeth.

Closest living relative

Just like Scutosaurus, they have bony armour, eat plants and move slowly.

Scutosaurus's heavy plates and short legs meant that they moved very slowly. They were one of the first vegetarian creatures too. They had to eat all the time, to be strong enough to carry their weight.

Inostrancevia

Scutosaurus

Moschops lived in Africa about 260 million years ago. Their most intriguing feature was their unique skull – about ten centimetres thick. That's ten times as thick as a human skull.

We think that when Moschops were fighting, they bashed their heads together. The thick skulls protected their brains, like helmets.

Moschops

Most of the creatures in this chapter became extinct in an extinction event 252 million years ago. This completely changed conditions around the world and left space for something new.

That something was dinosaurs, which survived for more than 170 million years. But this book isn't about them, so let's move on to what came afterwards.

 # Collecting fossils

Collecting fossils became very popular around 200 years ago, in the mid-1800s.

In 1823, Mary Anning found the first fossil of a huge prehistoric animal called a Plesiosaur. She made money for her family by selling fossils.

Plesiosaur

22

Stegosaurus

In 2024, a Stegosaurus skeleton sold for 44.6 million dollars. So fossils are still big business!

CHAPTER 3
Megafauna

When the dinosaurs became extinct, a lot of food was left for other creatures to eat.

In the era of the dinosaurs, mammals were small – the biggest ones weighed about ten kilograms. But without the dinosaurs around, some of the mammals got bigger … and bigger! So did some marine creatures, giving us megafauna, which means "really big animals".

The dinosaurs were already turning to fossils.

Titanoboa were colossal South American snakes, which lived about 60 million years ago. These enormous snakes could move on land and swim, and they lived mainly on fish.

Titanoboa

Titanoboa were about 13 metres long. That's about the same length as a single-decker bus.

The biggest land mammals ever were called Paraceratherium. They were about five metres tall, and weighed as much as four African elephants!

Paraceratherium were so tall that they could eat from the very tops of trees.

Paraceratherium

Closest living relative

Paraceratherium didn't have horns, but rhinos are their closest descendants.

Thirty million years later Paraceratherium fossils caused confusion for scientists.

People in different countries found Paraceratherium fossil parts, but the scientists thought that they came from different animals. These fossils were all given different names until the scientists worked together and agreed it was all the same animal.

Paraceratherium wasn't the only fossil to cause confusion. When scientists first found Basilosaurus, they thought they were reptiles. But Basilosaurus were actually early whales – they were just a really different shape from whales today.

Basilosaurus were about the size of humpback whales. They became extinct about 33 million years ago.

Basilosaurus

humpback whale

Basilosaurus's teeth were unusual too. Today's toothed whales have only one kind of teeth – they're sharp and pointed, to grip and rip up their prey. But Basilosaurus had more than one kind of teeth. Because the back teeth were worn down, we know Basilosaurus chewed their prey.

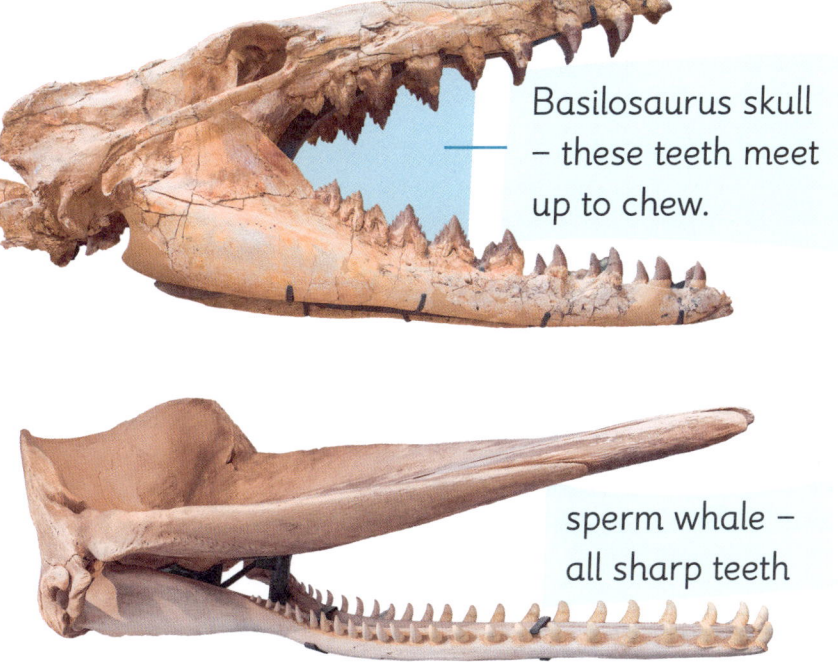

Basilosaurus skull – these teeth meet up to chew.

sperm whale – all sharp teeth

Pristichampsus was another fossil that challenged scientists.

At first, scientists thought that Pristichampsus looked a lot like today's crocodiles, but with much longer legs. Scientists decided that these longer, stronger legs helped Pristichampsus to move around better on land.

But the more they thought about Pristichampsus, the less certain they became.

Remember scientists once thought that Paraceratherium were lots of different creatures? It was the other way round for Pristichampsus. Scientists are no longer convinced that all their fossils belong to one creature.

This is because they realised that most parts of Pristichampsus could fit into other creatures from the same time. So Pristichampsus might not be a real creature at all!

We do really know that there were enormous birds, as well as animals and sea creatures. These huge prehistoric 'terror birds' lived in South America from about 53 million years ago.

All of these birds had big, strong, curved beaks and flexible necks. They probably killed their prey by chopping at it with their beak.

terror bird

These birds were so successful that they even spread into North America.

They had long legs and only small wings, so most of them didn't fly at all – but they were good runners. Scientists think that the fastest ones could run up to 48 kilometres per hour. That's over five times as fast as most humans can run!

Mistakes with fossils

Scientists first put together an Iguanodon with a horn like a rhino's – until they found a more complete fossil. This showed the 'horn' was a claw.

horn

claw

Anomalocaris was similar – scientists thought at first that they had big, long front legs.

But when they found a whole fossil, scientists realised the 'legs' really belonged on Anomalocaris's head. They were long, grabby feelers that Anomalocaris used to catch other creatures to eat!

CHAPTER 4

Living with humans

Humans evolved over 300,000 years ago, but all the creatures you've read about so far were extinct before then. So what was on Earth when humans appeared?

This chapter is about the megafauna that we know lived alongside early humans. There were small animals too, of course, but these big ones were particularly extraordinary!

Megalania lived in Australia from about 300,000 years ago and became extinct about 40,000 years ago. We're not sure exactly how big these enormous lizards were, because we've never found a complete skeleton. But their bones were really big.

Megalania

Closest living relative

Today's monitor lizards have sharp teeth and **venomous** spit, just like Megalania.

37

More about ... estimating the size of creatures

If scientists find a complete skeleton, it's easy to know how big the creature was.

But if they don't, they have to make educated guesses, based on how big the bones are. This can be a good guide to the creature's size.

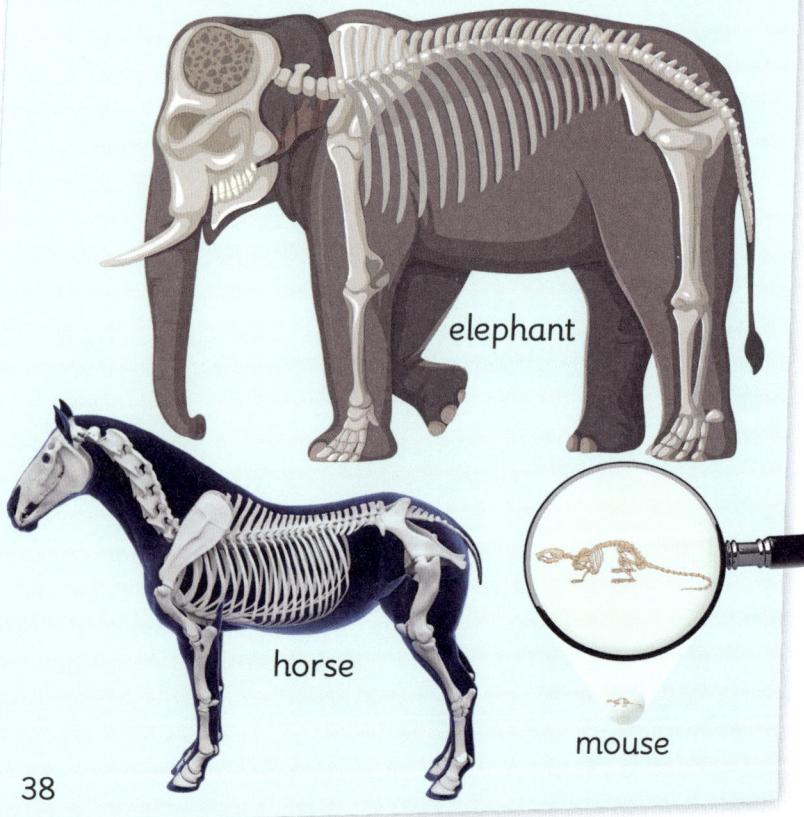

elephant

horse

mouse

Megalania were scaly reptiles, but
the most famous creatures from this time
are probably the woolly mammoth and
the woolly rhino. We call them woolly,
but they didn't actually have wool – they
were furry!

They needed this thick fur to keep them
warm, because they lived in northern areas,
in an era when the weather was cold.

Woolly rhinos fed on grass and shrubs, and woolly mammoths used their tusks to dig roots out of the frozen ground.

But as the weather warmed up, it caused problems for both creatures. First it got snowy, so grass wouldn't grow and woolly rhinos died out. As it warmed further, the woolly mammoths' thick fur meant they couldn't cool down, so they died out too.

We have evidence that early humans saw woolly mammoths and woolly rhinos.

We can tell that early humans hunted them, because some of the bones we have found have knife marks on them.

Early humans made statues and cave paintings of both creatures as well.

Megatherium were distant relations of today's tree sloths – but they were much bigger. They were up to five metres tall – that's almost as tall as a house – and they weighed about the same as elephants. They lived on the ground, as they were probably just too big to climb trees!

Megatherium

Scientists can tell from Megatherium fossils that their legs were better for walking than running. But we don't know if they moved as slowly as the sloths we have today. They lived on grass as well as eating leaves.

Different kinds of Megatherium lived in North and South America.

Closest living relative

two-toed sloth

Megatherium

There were huge birds too, including the unique Madagascan elephant bird. These birds didn't have trunks – but they were about as tall as an elephant. They lived on the island of Madagascar and they were the biggest birds ever.

Elephant birds died out only about 1,000 years ago.

Experts have found elephant bird skeletons, and lots of pieces of their eggshells.
The eggs were huge – if you made up a complete shell from the pieces, you could fit about 150 chicken eggs inside it!

There are two whole giant fossil eggs in Australia. They washed up on the coast, over 7,000 kilometres from the birds' home.

chicken egg

elephant bird egg

BONUS

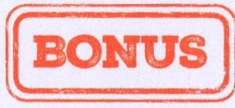

Today's megafauna

We still have some enormous animals today. Here are some of them and where they are in the world.

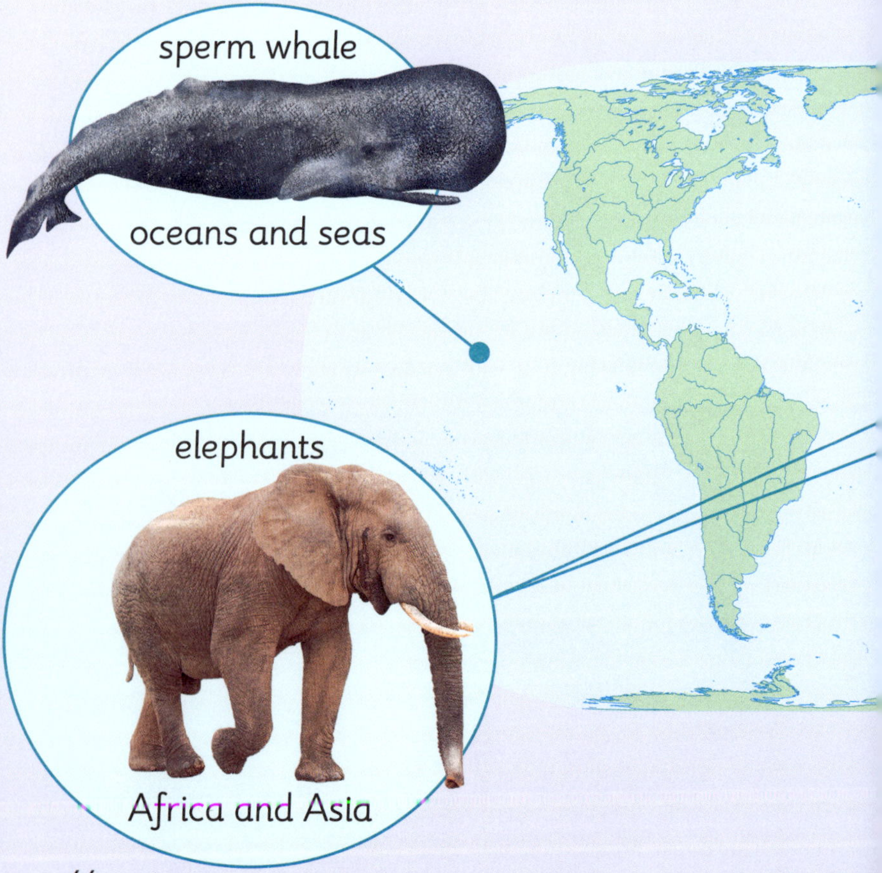
sperm whale
oceans and seas
elephants
Africa and Asia

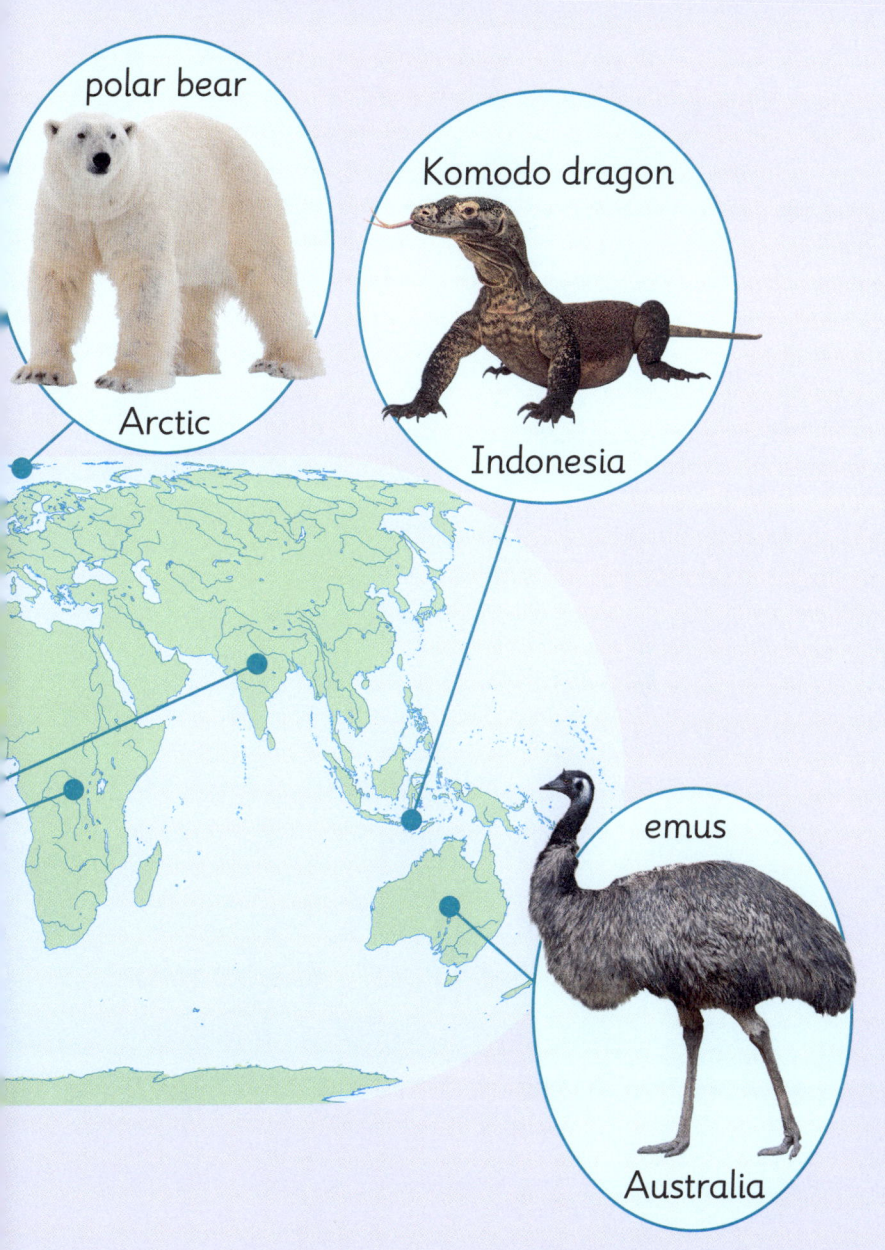

polar bear

Arctic

Komodo dragon

Indonesia

emus

Australia

In human times

The biggest extinctions happened millions of years ago. But this chapter is about creatures that have become extinct more recently.

Humans are certainly to blame for some of these extinctions, because of farming practices or hunting. Sometimes, animals came to a new place with humans. These animals caused extinctions in their new homes, by being better at getting food than the local creatures.

Farming was probably what made aurochs extinct. Aurochs were a kind of cow, which evolved thousands of years before humans.

Early humans hunted aurochs and then bred them to create the cows we have today. Gradually, cows took over. Aurochs became more and more scarce, until they became extinct.

This picture of an aurochs was painted about 17,000 years ago in a cave in France.

Thylacines lived in Australia for over 18 million years. But then they became extinct because of humans bringing another animal into the area.

About 5,000 years ago, some humans sailed to Australia with a kind of dog called a dingo. Dingoes lived on the same kinds of food as thylacines, but they were better at getting it.

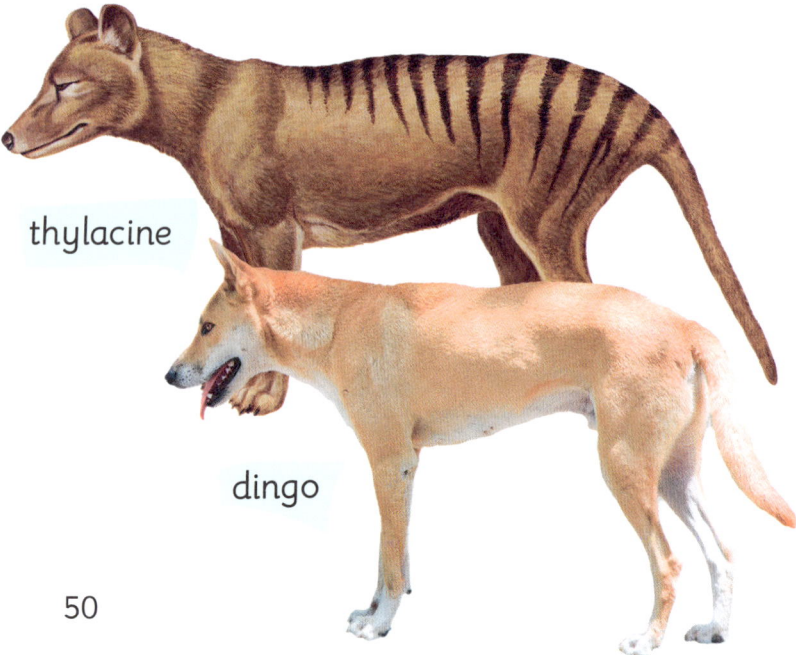

thylacine

dingo

Because of this, thylacines became extinct in Australia about 2,000 years ago.

Luckily, there were no dingoes on the Australian island of Tasmania. So 5,000 or so thylacines survived there until humans came to the island.

The settlers called them 'Tasmanian tigers' because of their stripy coat.

But when people started farming on Tasmania, they thought the thylacines would kill their farm animals. So farmers started hunting them. Thylacines became completely extinct in 1936.

Thylacines looked like dogs, but they were actually **marsupials**, like kangaroos. Like them, thylacines had pouches for their young to grow in.

Closest living relatives

Thylacines' closest relatives are other **carnivorous** marsupials. These include Tasmanian devils, which are extinct on the Australian mainland, but still live in Tasmania. They're about half the size of thylacines.

Numbats are a lot smaller, but their stripy coats mean they look most like thylacines.

Humans were directly to blame for quaggas becoming extinct. Quaggas were a kind of South African zebra, with fewer stripes than the zebras you see today. Their back end had no stripes at all.

People thought quaggas were so beautiful, they started collecting quagga skins. So many collectors wanted them, they hunted quaggas to extinction. People tried to save quaggas by keeping them in zoos, but the last one died in 1883.

quagga

You've certainly heard of dodos,
the turkey-sized, flightless birds that lived
on Madagascar. Everything was fine for
them until sailing ships came in the 1600s.

Some dodos were eaten by hungry sailors,
but that wasn't the main problem. Rats, dogs
and monkeys also came on
the ships. These animals fed
on the food the dodos needed –
and the dodos' eggs too.
So almost as soon as humans
found out about dodos,
dodos became extinct.

Dodos became famous because of how quickly they became extinct. So although it's been hundreds of years since anyone saw a live dodo, there are pictures of them around the world. This cafeteria in Belarus has one on its sign, for example.

We still say things are "as dead as a dodo". Dodos have become a symbol of extinction – a reason for people to work against creatures becoming extinct.

CHAPTER 6

Back from the brink

Animals are still at risk of extinction. But this chapter is about some creatures we are managing to save.

Sea otters have fur so thick that they stay dry and warm, even in the cold sea. People started hunting them about 300 years ago, to get their fur for coats. They hunted until there were fewer than 2,000 sea otters in the world.

Hunting sea otters has been banned for over 50 years, since 1972. Scientists have reintroduced sea otters to areas where they used to live. Now there are about 130,000 of them around the world.

Sea otters are not only beautiful – they are clever. They use rocks to break open shellfish to eat, while floating on their backs in the water.

Like sea otters, beavers were once hunted for their fur. There were thousands in the UK, but they were extinct there by the 1500s.

Beavers are seriously useful animals, because they look after the rivers and ponds where they live. So in 2009, **conservationists** started reintroducing them to the UK.

Beavers improve the watery areas they live in, by cutting down trees, building dams and digging channels.

Once they were reintroduced into the UK, it became clear how helpful their activity was. The areas where they now live have clearer water, more wildlife, and the rivers are much less likely to burst their banks.

Another animal brought back from the brink is the golden lion tamarin which lives in the Brazilian rainforest. These little monkeys are cat-sized and very light. They jump and scramble around the trees, eating fruit, flowers, eggs and insects. Their long fingers are brilliant at digging things out of tiny spaces.

In the 1970s, there were scarcely 200 of them.

This is because people were hunting the tamarins. People also cut down many rainforest trees, to get wood and make space for digging mines. This left the tamarins with fewer places to live.

But golden lion tamarins have been reintroduced from zoos, and their areas are being protected. Now there are about 3,200 of them in the wild.

Black-footed ferrets
became scarce in
North America, after
people started farming on
the land where they lived.

black-footed ferret

Black-footed ferrets mainly eat
prairie dogs. But the prairie dogs damaged
the farmers' crops. So the farmers killed off
all the prairie dogs. Once their food was
gone, people thought the ferrets
must be extinct.

prairie dog

Somehow, some black-footed ferrets survived. Now the ferrets have been reintroduced, and the farmers are sharing the land with them. They are finding new ways to keep prairie dogs off their crops.

There are about 370 black-footed ferrets in the wild now. Experts will feel they are safe once there are about 3,000 of them.

Millions of creatures have become extinct throughout the history of the world. Many creatures are **endangered** today too. Farming, hunting, and changing weather patterns all pose a risk to wildlife, from frogs and butterflies to pandas.

But people are working all over the planet to help save creatures from extinction.

This conservation work involves protecting important places like rainforests and coral reefs, which are home to many extraordinary, unique creatures.

The first step to helping endangered creatures is being interested in them and their stories. Let's make sure we enjoy and protect all the amazing creatures in our world!

65

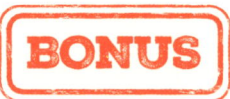

BONUS Where they live

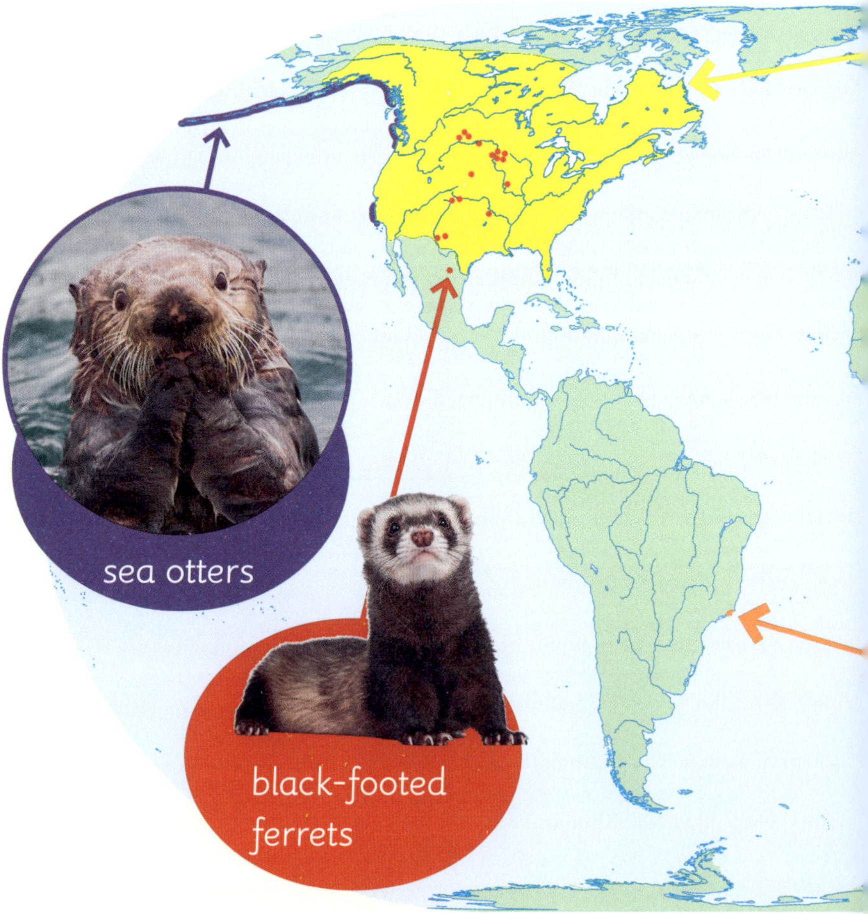
sea otters
black-footed ferrets

beavers

golden lion
tamarins

Glossary

asteroid a small rocky object that travels through space

carnivorous meat-eating

conservationists people who work to help keep nature healthy or to improve it

endangered threatened with extinction

evolved developed over thousands of years

fossils the remains of a creature, or the shape of it, preserved in stone

mammals creatures that have live young and make milk for them

marine belonging to the sea

marsupials mammals that have a pouch which their young live in for the first months of their life

philosopher a deep thinker

reptiles creatures which have scales and
    cannot keep themselves warm

seabed the ground under the sea

venomous containing a poison that can hurt
    or kill what it's bitten

wetlands an area of ponds, marshes
    and streams

About the author

Why did you want to be an author?

I've always loved reading – I even used to pretend to read books before I could. Once I understood that people actually write books, that was what I wanted to do. The opportunity to write books that make people want to read – that seems to me the best thing in the world!

Becca Heddle

How did you start writing?

I started writing for myself when I was about seven. I love words and how they fit together. Later, I worked in a bookshop and then for a publisher. Finally, I got to write books myself.

What do you like best about writing?

I love it when I've written my first draft. I can start to see the shape of the book, and get an idea of how it might work for the reader.

Where do you like to write?

I like writing on trains best of all. It's a special space where you're travelling along, apart from the rest of your life – perfect for getting ideas flowing.

How do you go about writing a non-fiction book like this?

I read and read, until I can find a way in – an idea that just makes my brain tingle with excitement. Once I started researching extinct animals, I realised how much there was to learn. I didn't come up for days! And then I write, and rewrite again and again, until I think I'm passing on that excitement.

What would you like readers to learn from this book?

That throughout the history of the world, astonishing creatures have become extinct. But each extinction makes space for more amazing life forms. And that we can help creatures threatened with extinction today.

Which creature in the book do you like best? Why?

I've always found woodlice really cute, so I love trilobites – they are like prehistoric, underwater woodlice! I love to picture them scuttling and swimming around for millions of years.

Which extinct creature would you bring back?

The griffinfly – at least when I'm writing this – it might be a different one tomorrow! I find dragonflies fascinating, and can't get my head around the idea of one that big. So I'd love to see one in real life. It might be a bit intimidating, though.

Book chat

Did you know what extinct meant before you read this book?

Have you read any other books like this?

Had you heard of any of these creatures before?

What was the most interesting thing you learnt from this book?

If you could go back in time and see any of these creatures, which would you visit?

Which animal in this book do you like the best and why?

Have you ever seen a fossil?

Have you ever seen any of these animals on TV or in museums?

Who would you recommend this book to and why?

If you could ask the author anything, what would you ask?

If you had to give this book a different title, what would it be?

Is there a creature in this book you'd like to learn more about?

Would you like to be a conservationist? Why or why not?

How would you sum up this book in one sentence?

Which creature would you bring back to life if you could and why?

Which picture in this book do you think is the best? Why?

Book challenge:

Choose any creature in this book to find out more about.

Collins
BIG CAT

Published by Collins An imprint of
HarperCollins*Publishers*

The News Building   Macken House
1 London Bridge Street   39/40 Mayor Street Upper
London   Dublin 1
SE1 9GF   D01 C9W8
UK   Ireland

© HarperCollins*Publishers* Limited 2025

10 9 8 7 6 5 4 3 2

ISBN 978-0-00-874633-9

British Library Cataloguing-in-Publication Data
A catalogue record for this publication is available
from the British Library.

Download the teaching notes and
word cards to accompany this book at:
http://littlewandle.org.uk/signupfluency/

Get the latest Collins Big Cat news at
collins.co.uk/collinsbigcat

Author: Becca Heddle
Publisher: Laura White
Product managers: Caroline Green and
          Holly Woolnough
Series editor: Charlotte Raby
Commissioning editor: Emily Hooton
Phonics consultant: Catherine Baker
Project manager: Emily Hooton
Copyeditor: Sally Byford
Proofreader: Catherine Dakin
Cover designer: Sarah Finan
Typesetter: 2Hoots Publishing Services Ltd
Production controller: Katharine Willard

Printed in the UK.

MIX
Paper | Supporting
responsible forestry
FSC
www.fsc.org   **FSC™ C007454**

This book contains FSC™ certified paper and other controlled
sources to ensure responsible forest management.

For more information visit: www.harpercollins.co.uk/green

Made with responsibly sourced
paper and vegetable ink

Scan to see how we are reducing
our environmental impact.

Acknowledgements
The publishers gratefully acknowledge the permission
granted to reproduce the copyright material in this
book. Every effort has been made to trace copyright
holders and to obtain their permission for the use of
copyright material. The publishers will gladly receive
any information enabling them to rectify any error or
omission at the first opportunity.

Front cover Trixy Gatto/Shutterstock, back cover
tl Catmando/Shutterstock, tr Warpaint/Shutterstock,
b Catmando/Shutterstock, p4 dotted zebra/Alamy,
p5 Elena Elenaphotos21/Alamy, p7 Stocktrek Images,
Inc./Alamy, p9 Ashley Cooper/Getty Images, p10 PB/
YB/Alamy, p12 dotted zebra/Alamy, p13 Aunt Spray /
Alamy, p14 Corbin17/Alamy, p17 Corey Ford/Alamy,
p21 YAY Media AS/Alamy, p22 Science History Images/
Alamy, p25 dotted zebra/Alamy, p26 mark Turner/
Alamy, p27 dave stamboulis /Alamy, p29b Endless
Travel/Alamy, p30t Larry Felder, National Park Service/
Wikimedia Commons, p30b DagdaMor/Wikimedia
Commons, p34t Maidun Collection/Alamy, p34b mark
Turner/Alamy, p41 Dominic Robinson/Alamy, p45
NATURAL HISTORY MUSEUM, LONDON/Science Photo
Library, p49 Hemis /Alamy, p50 & p52t Universal Images
Group North America LLC/Alamy, p52b Joel Sartore /
Photo Ark/Nature Picture Library, p53 Martin Camm /
Carwardine/Nature Picture Library, pp54–55 Stocktrek
Images, Inc./Alamy, p59 Robert McGouey/Wildlife/
Alamy, p60 BIOSPHOTO/Alamy, p63 Kerry Hargrove/
Alamy, p65t Douglas Carr/Alamy, p65b The Photolibrary
Wales/Alamy, p66b Niebrugge Images/Alamy.

All other photos Shutterstock.